THE
LITTLE RICE
BOOK

Judy Ridgway

PIATKUS

Other titles in the series

The Little Green Avocado Book
The Little Garlic Book
The Little Pepper Book
The Little Lemon Book
The Little Apple Book
The Little Strawberry Book
The Little Mushroom Book
The Little Nut Book
The Little Bean Book
The Little Honey Book
The Little Mustard Book

© 1984 Judy Piatkus (Publishers) Limited

First published in 1984 by Judy Piatkus
(Publishers) Limited of London

British Library Cataloguing in Publication Data
Ridgway, Judy
The little rice book.
1. Rice
I. Title
641.3′318 SB191.R5

ISBN 0-86188-469-8

Drawings by Linda Broad
Designed by Ken Leeder
Cover photograph by John Lee

Typeset by Gilbert Composing Services
Printed and bound by
Pitman Press, Bath

CONTENTS

RICE

Rice is one of the oldest cereal crops grown and it is also one of the most important. It forms the staple diet of over half the population of the world and is cultivated in countries as far afield as India and China, North and South America, Africa and also in Europe. Italy produces quite substantial quantities of rice and both Greece and France appear in the world production tables.

Rice is a natural convenience food. It does not require lengthy preparation and it can be cooked in as little as twelve to fifteen minutes. There is no wastage with rice and it will keep in the store cupboard for a year or more.

Versatility is also the keynote for rice and every country has its own special rice dishes. It can be served as an accompaniment to other dishes or it may form the basis of a main course dish in its own right. It can also be used in soups and salads, in stuffings and fillings and in all kinds of hot and cold puddings.

Rice is particularly easy to digest and this is why Westerners often feel hungry fairly soon after eating a rice-based meal. However it also means that it can be served to young and old alike as well as to people on special diets.

Punjabi saying: 'Fine rice, buffalo's milk, a good wife, white clothes; these are the four marks of heaven.'

HISTORY OF RICE

Some authorities trace the origin of rice to India but the earliest mention of rice in history was in 2800 BC when a Chinese emperor established a ceremonial rite for the planting of rice. By 2500 BC rice was well established in the valley of the Yangtze Kiang river and from there it spread to India and the rest of South-East Asia. In those days, with no fast means of transport and very little communication between different areas of the world, rice probably travelled with pilgrims walking slowly from country to country and perhaps with horse caravans or camel trains.

Rice was firmly established in the Middle East by 400 BC. It also found its way via Persia to Greece and the poet Sophocles mentioned rice in his tragedies. It was introduced to Southern Europe by the Arabs who cultivated it along the shores of the Mediterranean, in Sicily and later in lower Aragon in Spain. From there it eventually reached the Lombardy Plain of Italy where it is still grown today.

Rice was unknown in Britain until medieval times when the Crusaders came into contact with the Saracens. When it was first imported it was strictly for the rich. It came in on the spice ships and for many years was watched over and locked up with the precious spices in special spice boxes or chests.

One of the earliest European recipes using rice was 'rys Lombarde', a reference to the Italian origin of some of the rice. This was a savoury dish using spices and the yolks of hard-boiled eggs.

Rice featured in a number of special Lenten dishes and the Countess of Leicester and her family used a hundred and ten pounds of rice in the four months between Christmas and April 1265 and she paid about a penny ha'penny a pound for it. However, the Countess of Leicester's household was a large and relatively sophisticated one. The records for the much smaller household of Dame Alice de Bryene show that only three pounds of rice, costing one penny per pound, were consumed in the whole of the year from September 1418 to September 1419.

Rice in those days was boiled in an earthenware pot with stock and then flavoured with almond milk and saffron. On fish days the rice was cooked in almond milk alone and sweetened with sugar.

It was not until the seventeenth century that rice pudding came to be baked. In a typical recipe rice was first boiled with milk, then flavoured with nutmeg, mace, rosewater and sugar and mixed with eggs, breadcrumbs and marrow minced with ambergrise. It was then baked in a buttered dish. This rich concoction contrasts with the economical rice pudding of the next century. This was made by tying a quantity of rice and some currants loosely in a cloth and boiling them in plain water until the rice had swelled sufficiently. If the household was not too poor the dish was served with a little melted butter and sugar.

Rice was not introduced to America until the end of the seventeenth century. The story goes that in 1694 a ship sailing from Madagascar had to put into South Carolina for repairs. The Governor helped the Captain and in return was given some seeds of rice.

The seeds took to the new soil and quite soon Carolina was supplying not only its own demand for rice but also that of its neighbours and in due course that of its trading partners as well. Carolina rice was exported in some quantity and in the nineteenth century pudding or short grain rice was nearly always known as Carolina rice.

Savoury rice has been served with certain French and Italian dishes for centuries and the growth of Britain's Empire in the East also led to an increase in the amount of savoury rice eaten. Dishes such as kedgeree became traditional both on the middle-class breakfast table and in the stately home. However, the great upsurge of interest in Eastern food in the second half of the twentieth century has really established rice in the culinary repertoire.

RICE FACTS AND FIGURES

UK IMPORTS

Today most of the rice sold in the UK comes from America, though no longer from Carolina. Instead the rice comes from Louisiana, Texas, Arkansas, California and the Mississippi basin. A little rice is also imported from Italy and from India, but most Eastern countries need their crop for their own growing populations.

In 1983 Britain imported 183,492 tons of rice. Most of this was semi or wholly milled in the country of origin but 33,892 tons came in as brown rice and 13,225 tons as broken rice.

WORLD PRODUCTION

America produces over seven million tons of rice each year and has plenty to spare for export. But this quantity is only a tiny fraction of the 412 million tons produced in the world as a whole.

The largest producer is China with a huge 155 million tons. Their nearest rival is India with 68 million tons. Next comes Bangladesh with 21 million tons and Japan with 12 million tons.

The overall production figure for South America is 15 million tons with Brazil as the major producer, and in Africa the total production is nearly nine million tons with Nigeria leading the way.

The USSR produces two and a half million tons and Europe's output is nearly two millions tons. The major European producer is Italy with 900,000 tons. Greece produces 83,000 tons, and France a rather surprising 27,000 tons from the Carmargue.

Australia, too, contributes 850,000 tons to world stocks and Mexico 600,000 tons.

GROWING RICE

Water and heat are vital to a good rice crop, so rice grows best in those parts of the world where there is a high rainfall, a hot temperature and suitable soil. With the exception of upland rice which is cultivated much as other cereals, rice is grown on submerged land in coastal plains and river basins. Its growing season varies from three to eight months, and some countries have two or three crops a year.

Most rice is grown in flat fields or paddies which need to be flooded, and it takes an amazing 300 gallons of water to grow only one pound of rice. In the more primitive countries much of the irrigation is left to chance and to the weather.

The cultivation of rice in most countries is a back-breaking job. First of all the land has to be farrowed. This is followed by the hand sowing of the rice seed in prepared beds. After 25–50 days the seedlings are transplanted to the paddies. Here they remain submerged in two to four inches of water throughout the growing period. When the rice plant reaches about four feet in height it is ready to be harvested.

By contrast, rice growing in the more advanced countries of the world is a highly mechanised process with air-conditioned tractors to prepare the land, aeroplanes to sow the seeds and a complicated permanent system of dams and channels to irrigate the fields.

Rice in the husk can be dried on the stalk before threshing or it can be partially dried before threshing and then spread thinly on the ground to finish drying. Paddy rice can also be threshed first and then spread to dry in the fresh air and sunshine. These simple methods unfortunately result in a larger number of cracked grains which will break in milling. In the USA the rice is dried in electronically-controlled dryers using quite high temperatures. Modern drying methods have greatly increased the quality of rice but they are very expensive to install.

PROCESSING RICE

Dried paddy rice needs careful milling to make it edible. The first step is to clean the rice, removing pieces of mud, leaves, stalks, and the like. The next step is to shell the rice to remove the non-edible husk which covers every grain. When this has been done the result is brown rice. The majority of this edible brown rice is processed even further and the bran removed to produce milled or polished rice.

In the rural districts and villages of most developing countries these processes are carried out by hand. A pestle and mortar are used to remove the husk and the bran. This method is slow and inefficient and nowadays is used only in those parts of the world where rice is grown mainly for home use.

Some developing countries have been able to install small to medium size cone mills. This is the simplest type of machinery and involves rubbing the grains of rice between a heavy carborundum wheel and a wire mesh sieve which automatically separates the milled rice from the husks and bran. The grains are then graded according to size.

In the industrial countries, large and expensive mills with the latest equipment ensure that the rice is likely to be of a superior quality; less starchy and with fewer broken grains.

'With coarse rice to eat, with water to drink and my bended arm for a pillow.'

Confucius 551–476 BC

FOOD VALUE OF RICE

Rice is a great energy producer. It is made up largely of starch or carbohydrate. However, this does not mean that it is necessarily fattening. It contains only half the calories as the same amount of bread. For the calorie conscious 3 oz of cooked rice contains about 77 calories.

The particular type of starch found in rice is very easily and quickly digested. It only requires about an hour of digestion compared with most other foods which require anything from two to four hours.

Rice also contains a surprisingly high level of protein. When this protein is served with other foods such as milk, beans or peas the amino acids of the two foods combine to give a greater nutritive value than would be achieved if the foods were eaten separately.

There is very little fat in rice which is good news for those on a low fat diet. However, frying the rice will increase the fat content of the finished dish quite substantially. An alternative is to mix all the ingredients for a fried rice dish, excluding the fat, and to bake it, using the oven cooking method given on page 22. Remember to boil the water or stock before adding to the dish.

Some people suffer from food allergies and need to watch their diets carefully. For this group rice and rice products are ideal, for they have never been known to cause allergic reactions. It is also gluten-free and is thus suitable for coeliacs and those on a gluten-free diet.

Brown rice contains useful quantitites of phosphorous potassium and the B vitamins, mostly found in the germ of the rice, which is unfortunately lost when it is milled. However, parboiled rice does retain more of these nutrients than does ordinary rice. The level of calcium is high in all types of rice and they are all equally low in natural salt or sodium.

The loss of the B vitamins in milled rice is one of the causes of beri-beri in countries where rice is the staple food. However in a mixed diet there is no problem.

COMPOSITION OF RICE

(Average values in 100 grams/3½oz cooked rice)

	Brown rice	White rice	Parboiled rice
protein (g)	2.5	2.0	2.1
fat (g)	0.6	0.1	0.1
carbohydrate (g)	25.5	24.2	23.3
fibre	0.3	0.1	0.1
calcium (mg)	12	10	19
phosphorous (mg)	73	28	57
potassium (mg)	70	28	43
thiamine (mg)	0.09	0.02	0.05
riboflavin (mg)	0.02	0.01	0.01
niacin (mg)	1.4	0.4	1.2

CHOOSING RICE

There are a number of different kinds of rice on sale in the shops and it is important to choose the right kind of rice for the right culinary job.

SHORT GRAIN OR PUDDING RICE

The grains are chalky in colour and have a tubby look. They are only about twice as long as they are wide. When they are cooked they tend to stick together and this makes them ideal for puddings and sweets. This is the kind of rice which used to be known as Carolina rice.

GLUTINOUS RICE

In the Far East there is another type of short grain rice which is even more glutinous and sticky than pudding rice. It is used in Congee, a kind of Chinese rice gruel, and in a variety of Japanese dishes, as stuffings or dumplings. It is available in this country in specialist food shops.

MEDIUM GRAIN OR RISOTTO RICE

Here the grains are two to three times as long as they are wide and they are less chalky and more translucent than pudding rice. When cooked they are less sticky but they do still mould together.

This kind of rice is used mainly for risottos, stuffings, croquettes and also for rice puddings of various kinds. The best type of Italian risotto rice is Arborio.

LONG GRAIN RICE

This is sometimes known as Patna rice after one of the most popular Indian varieties. The grains are very long and slim and are four to five times as long as they are wide. The best long grain rice is not chalky but translucent in colour.

Properly cooked long grain rice has a light fluffy texture, and the grains remain quite separate. This is why it is preferred as the accompaniment to savoury dishes. It can also be safely used for almost any recipe which calls for rice. It takes about 15 minutes to cook.

When choosing long grain rice examine the pack carefully and avoid any with a high proportion of broken or chalky looking grains. Broken grains result in uneven cooking and chalkiness means excess starch and therefore stickiness.

Basmati rice is another Indian long grain rice, which is grown in the Himalayan region and is considered to have the finest flavour. It has the longest grains and can be quite expensive. It takes about the same time to cook as Patna rice.

BROWN RICE

This is rice which has only had the outer husk removed. Most of the bran and the germ are still intact. The rice looks darker in colour and has a coarser, more nutty texture and flavour. It has a much higher vitamin and mineral content than ordinary milled white rice. Because of its coarser texture it takes longer to cook, usually around 20–25 minutes. It is available in both long and short grain varieties.

PRE-COOKED RICE

This is instant rice. After milling, the rice is cooked, or in some instances half cooked, and then dehydrated. The only preparation necessary afterwards is to put back the moisture which was removed during drying. Follow the instructions on the pack for the best results.

'He who has wheat, also wants rice.'
Russian proverb

PARBOILED RICE

This is a process which was developed in the USA during World War II. It results in rice which is said to be easier to cook and to contain more of the nutrients that are usually lost when the rice is milled.

The process involves soaking the paddy or unhusked rice in hot water. This does not involve cooking the rice and parboiled rice is quite different to pre-cooked rice. The water is then drained away and high pressure steam applied.

During this treatment the soluble nutrients in the bran layers and the germ of the rice go into solution and the steam spreads the nutritional elements uniformly throughout the entire kernel. The processed rice is then dried, shelled and milled in the usual way. The starch in the rice is gelatinised and the treatment hardens the grain. This means that parboiled rice needs a slightly longer cooking time than ordinary rice. The cooked grains are separate and fluffy and the cooked yield is higher.

There are variations in the process and these give the rice different colours and flavours. In some countries parboiled rice has a very strong odour but this is not acceptable in the West. Parboiled rice also looks yellower in colour than plain rice but this colour difference disappears in cooking.

'Rice obtained by crookedness will not boil up into good food.' Chinese proverb

WILD RICE

This is really a misnomer for wild rice is quite unrelated to cultivated rice and is not even a true grain. It is the seed of a wild grass which thrives in Northern Minnesota in the USA. Eighty per cent of all wild rice grown comes from here and the remainder from certain parts of Canada and Wisconsin.

The seeds grow in lakes or streams and eventually thrust up floating leaves and stalks with the grain which stands well above the surface of the water.

Wild rice was once a staple food of the Sioux and Chippewa Indians and is still harvested in the traditional Indian way by Indian workers in canoes.

A state law was passed to ban all mechanical harvesting devices to safeguard the Indians' revenue.

The dark-coloured grain is surrounded by a husk which is removed. It is richer in protein, carbohydrates, minerals and B vitamins than cultivated rice and is much more expensive.

Before cooking it should be washed and soaked for several hours. Wild rice requires three times its volume of boiling water, plus salt for cooking. It needs to be simmered for 35–40 minutes until all the water is absorbed. Because of its cost it is often mixed with six to seven parts brown rice.

RICE FLOWER

This too has nothing to do with cultivated rice. It is an evergreen flowering shrub to be found in Australia. It is a hot-house plant and grows to be about three feet in height. There are both pink and white flowering varieties.

RICE PRODUCTS

Only about 50 per cent of every sack of paddy rice ends up as the whole grain rice sold in the supermarket. Ten per cent of it is bran which with other parts of rice is used to feed animals. Rice oil, extracted from bran, is used in margarine, some soap and for the treatment of leather.

A further 20 per cent are husks and these are used for fuel or in the manufacture of packing materials and abrasives.

The remaining 20 per cent consists of broken grains from which we get flaked rice, ground rice, rice flour and the cereal rice crispies.

FLAKED RICE

Flaked rice looks very like rolled oats and can be used in very much the same way to make a sweet or savoury porridge or milk pudding. It can also be used as a coating for rissoles and croquettes and for biscuits and crunchy toppings for casseroles and puddings.

GROUND RICE

This is a kind of coarse rice flour similar in texture to semolina. It can, indeed, be used in much the same way as semolina to make a thick milk pudding. It is also used in other confectionary such as shortbread, maids of honour and sandcake.

RICE FLOUR

This is similar to ground rice but is ground very much finer. One of its uses is to replace wheat flour in cakes and breads for those who have an allergy to the gluten in wheat. It is also used in Chinese cooking to make dumpling wrappers and rice noodles.

Rice flour is also used in pet foods and in face powder and other cosmetics. The heavy white make up used in Chinese opera owes a lot to rice flour.

PUFFED RICE

Usually sold as a breakfast cereal, the rice is heated and allowed to explode, and is then toasted and sweetened. This process puffs the rice to several times its original size, but removes all the vitamins, which are added later.

HOW MUCH RICE?

Rice expands by at least three times its own volume on cooking and so you only need quite small quantities of uncooked rice.

Generally speaking 2 oz or half a tea cup per person of uncooked rice will be sufficient for most purposes. Parboiled rice expands even more than ordinary rice and so slightly less will be required.

Here is a guide to the quantitites of uncooked rice required for four people for various types of dishes.

Rice dish as a starter	5–6 oz
Rice in a salad	4 oz
Rice as one of two accompaniments to the main course	6 oz
Rice as the main accompaniment	8 oz
Rice as a small part of the main dish	4–8 oz
Rice as the main constituent of the dish	10 oz
Rice in a dessert	3–4 oz
Rice pudding	$1\frac{1}{2}$–2 oz

BUFFETS

If you are including rice as part of a buffet meal use a little less rice, for people do not usually help themselves to very large quantities.

For 25 people	allow	1½–2 lbs
For 50 people	allow	3½–4 lbs
For 100 people	allow	7–8 lbs

COOKING RICE

There are probably as many methods of cooking rice as there are countries growing it. However the following methods are the simplest. They are also virtually foolproof.

BOILED RICE

For perfect fluffy long grain rice, all you need to do is to simmer the rice in twice its own volume of water in a tightly lidded pan until the grains have swollen up and absorbed all the water. The length of time this takes will depend upon the type of rice you are using.

There is usually no need to wash or soak rice unless it looks as if it might be rather dirty. Valuable vitamins and minerals can be lost by unnecessary washing. Soaking may also change the ratio of liquid needed to cook the rice.

STEP-BY-STEP GUIDE TO PERFECT BOILED RICE

1. Measure the rice.
2. Place double the same volume of water in a saucepan. Add some salt and the rice.
3. Bring to the boil, stir once and cover with a lid.
4. After 15 minutes* test the rice to see that it is tender and all the liquid has been removed. Fluff up with a fork.

**NEVER LIFT THE LID DURING
THE COOKING
AND
NEVER ATTEMPT TO STIR THE RICE
WHILE IT IS COOKING**

Very small quantities of rice may take a little less time and larger quantities a little longer. Parboiled and brown rice will also take longer so check the instructions on the pack.

OVEN-BAKED RICE

It is just as easy to cook rice in the oven. This method also saves fuel, particularly if you are planning to serve the rice with a dish which is cooked in the oven. Apply the basic proportions of twice the volume of liquid to rice.

Heat the liquid and place all the ingredients in a casserole. Stir once, cover with a lid and cook at 180C/350F/Gas 4 for 40–50 minutes. Test the rice to see that it is tender and all the liquid has been absorbed. Fluff up with a fork.

'Chattering does not cook the rice.' Hansa Proverb from Northern Nigeria

FRIED RICE

There are two versions of fried rice. In the Middle East and in India the rice is fried before it is cooked. Use cooking oil or a mixture of cooking oil and butter and fry the rice until it turns transparent. The proportion of rice and liquid are still the same as those given above, and once the rice has been fried the method is the same as for boiled rice.

In China, Malaysia and Indonesia the rice is fried after it has been cooked and left to cool. Boil the rice in the usual way and turn the cooked rice into a colander. Toss it with a fork from time to time as it cools. This will ensure really dry rice for frying.

Very often the frying is done in a Chinese curved wok but a large frying pan can also be used, and the rice is fried with a variety of ingredients.

'Even the clever daughter-in-law finds it hard to cook without rice.' Chinese Proverb

SERVING RICE

Certain classic dishes such as Scampi Provençale and Chicken à la King are served on a bed of rice. Others are served with rice on the side.

RICE MOULDS

This is an attractive way of serving rice. Simply cook the rice in the usual way. When it is cooked mix with 1 oz melted butter and spoon into individual dariole moulds which have been well greased. Press the rice well down and leave to stand for five minutes. Place heated plates over the top of moulds, invert and turn out, and serve with casseroles or grilled or fried meats.

Alternatively the cooked rice may be mixed with 2 beaten eggs and pressed into a greased ring mould. Place the ring mould in a baking tin filled with one inch of hot water. Bake at 180C/350F/Gas 4 for 40 minutes until set. Turn out to serve. Decorate with cooked vegetables in the centre or round the outside.

KEEPING RICE HOT

I deally rice should be served within ten minutes of cooking. However, you can keep rice warm for up to an hour in a covered pan, if you fluff up the rice and remove it from direct heat. Wrap the pan in hot towels or keep in a warm place.

If you want to keep rice hot for a longer period, place in a colander over hot water and cover with a lid or a towel. Alternatively undercook the rice and leave in a pan with a little water and some butter and finish cooking just before serving.

REHEATING COOKED RICE

Reheat cold rice by placing in a pan with a few tablespoons of water warmed over a moderate heat and shake the pan occasionally until the rice is heated through. With a good quality rice the result should be just as good as when freshly cooked.

STORING RICE

UNCOOKED RICE

Uncooked rice keeps for a year or more. Store in a cool, dark place.

COOKED RICE

Cooked rice may be kept for up to a week in a covered container in the fridge and for up to six months in a sealed container in the freezer. Thaw at room temperature before reheating.

If rice is frozen with other foods in risottos and pilafs it will have a much shorter life in the fridge and will only keep for about three months in the freezer.

FLAVOURING RICE

LIQUID FLAVOURINGS

Rice does not have a very strong flavour of its own and it will absorb other flavours very easily. Thus all kinds of different liquids can be used to cook the rice and change its flavour, and the rice can absorb the nutritional value of the liquid in which it is cooked. Because all the liquid is absorbed during cooking nothing is lost in the cooking process.

In place of water try:

*Chicken or beef stock.
*Canned consommé for an even stronger flavour.
*Vegetarians might use a yeast extract and hot water
   stock.

*Milk or coconut milk. The latter can either be made
  with desiccated coconut or with coconut cream.
*Equal quantities of tomato juice and water. Add a
  dash of Worcestershire Sauce.
*Equal quantities of orange juice and water with a
  pinch of coriander.

SOLID FLAVOURINGS

All kinds of herbs, spices, chopped vegetables, fruit
and nuts can be cooked with the rice to give it added
flavour. Limit the amount of added ingredients to 25
per cent of the rice cooked.
  Try:

*Powdered saffron or turmeric. Add butter and
  flaked almonds when the rice is cooked.
*Finely chopped onion and whole cumin seeds or
  curry powder.
*Freshly chopped parsley and mint plus chopped
  chives or a spring onion.
*A thick slice of lemon. Remove when the rice is
  cooked and fluff up with butter.
*Finely chopped spring onions and a little grated
  fresh root ginger.
*Finely chopped onions and some frozen peas.
*Mixed raisins, chopped nuts and candied peel.
*Chopped dried apricots.
*Finely chopped onion and green or red pepper with
  cayenne or paprika.
*Frozen mixed diced vegetables.

EASTERN RICE DISHES

CHINESE TASTY RICE

This is a meal in itself, but it can also be served, in smaller quantities, with other Chinese dishes.

8 oz can bamboo shoots
2 sticks celery, sliced
1 tablespoon soya sauce
3 tablespoons cooking oil
1 lb cooked rice, cold and fairly dry
7½ oz can button mushrooms diced
4 oz Chinese barbecued pork or cooked ham, diced
2 eggs, beaten
black pepper

Drain the liquid from the bamboo shoots into a saucepan and dice the bamboo shoots. Add to the pan with the celery and soya sauce. Bring to boil and simmer for 5 minutes.

Pour the cooking oil in a large frying pan or wok and fry the rice for 2 minutes. Add the mushrooms, pork or ham and egg and stir fry until the egg has set and the dish is hot. Drain the bamboo shoots and celery and add to the mixture. Sprinkle with black pepper and serve.

Serves 4–6

NASI GORENG WITH PEANUT SAUCE

This is the Indonesian version of fried rice. It is usually served with Peanut Sauce and you could add a green side salad.

14 fl oz chicken stock
2 oz creamed coconut
8 oz long grain rice
salt
3 eggs
1 tablespoon water
2½ tablespoons cooking oil
1 clove garlic, finely chopped
1 large onion, finely chopped
2 chicken breasts, boned and cut into thin strips
1 red pepper, seeded and finely chopped
1 teaspoon ground turmeric
¼ teaspoon ground ginger
4 oz frozen peas
4 oz peeled prawns
¼ pint stock

Heat the chicken stock in a pan and stir in the creamed coconut. Add the rice and salt and bring to the boil. Reduce the heat, cover and simmer for 12–15 minutes until all the liquid has been taken up and the rice is fluffy. Allow to cool.

Beat the eggs and water together. Heat 1 teaspoon oil in a frying pan and pour in the beaten egg. Spread out round the pan and cook until set. Remove to a plate, cut into strips and keep warm.

Pour 2 tablespoons of cooking oil in a very large frying pan or wok and fry the garlic and onion until the onion has softened. Add the chicken strips and stir fry until all traces of pink have disappeared from the flesh. Next stir in the red pepper, turmeric and ginger.

Stir fry for a further minute and add the peas, prawns, cold rice and stock. Cook for 5 minutes, stirring constantly. Serve with the egg strips laid on top of the rice and with Peanut Sauce on the side.

Serves 4

PEANUT SAUCE

4 oz peanut butter, smooth or crunchy
2 oz creamed coconut
juice of ½ lemon
1 tablespoon soya sauce
2 teaspoons curry powder
½ teaspoon chilli powder
½ pint water (or water and milk)

Mix all the ingredients except the water together in a small pan. Gradually add the water over a low heat until the sauce is smooth and hot.

Serves 4

CHIRASHIZUSHI

This is a Japanese dish which is traditionally served cold, but you could heat it in a wok and serve hot. All kinds of other ingredients—fish and vegetables—may be substituted for those used here. Serve as an unusual starter.

4 dried mushrooms
8 fl oz water
1 piece kelp (seaweed) if available
4 oz long grain rice
2 tablespoons vinegar
1/4 teaspoon salt
2 teaspoons sugar
2 eggs, beaten
knob of butter
1 small carrot, cut into sticks
1 oz green peas
1 oz French beans or broad beans, cut into sticks
1 oz lotus root or bamboo shoot (optional)
2 tablespoons soya sauce
2 oz peeled prawns

Soak the mushrooms in hot water until soft. Drain and cut into strips. Place 8 fl oz water and the kelp in a pan and bring to the boil. Remove the kelp and add the rice. Return to the boil, cover and simmer for 12–15 minutes until all the liquid has been absorbed and the rice is fluffy. Remove from the heat and leave to stand for 10 minutes. Heat the vinegar, salt and 1 teaspoon of the sugar in a small pan and pour over the rice. Mix together well with cutting strokes and fan the rice at the same time.

Fry the beaten eggs in a little butter to make a flat omelette. Cut into strips and then into small squares. Keep on one side.

Place the carrot sticks, peas, beans and lotus or bamboo shoot in a saucepan and just cover with water. Add the soya sauce and the remaining sugar and bring to the boil. Simmer for 5 minutes. Leave to cool. Drain and mix into the rice with the egg squares and all the remaining ingredients.

Serves 4

'There was an old man of Tobago,
Who lived on rice, gruel and sago,
Till, much to his bliss,
His physician said this,
To a leg, Sir, of mutton you may go!'

John Marshal in
Anecdotes and Adventures of 15 Gentlemen,
c. 1882 possibly by R.S. Sharpe

SEAFOOD PULAO

If you use prawns, they do not need to be cooked with the spices for as long as the cod.

2 tablespoons cooking oil
4 tablespoons freshly chopped coriander or parsley
2 teaspoons garam masala or curry powder
1 teaspoon turmeric
¼ teaspoon chilli powder
1 tablespoon lemon juice
12 oz fresh or smoked cod, filleted and cut into pieces, or
    12 oz peeled prawns
1 onion, finely chopped
8 oz long grain rice
16 fl oz water
salt and black pepper

Heat the oil in a saucepan and fry all the herbs and spices for a minute or so. Add the lemon juice and bring to the boil. Fry the fish in this mixture for about 3 minutes on each side. Remove from the pan and keep on one side.

Add the onion to the pan and stir over a medium heat and then add the rice, the water and seasoning. Bring to the boil, stir and cover. Cook for 10 minutes. Place the pieces of fish on top of the rice and cook for a further 15 minutes over a very low heat. Stir once and remove from the heat but keep in a warm place for 10 minutes before serving.

Serves 4

RICE WITH LENTILS

In some parts of the Middle East this dish is known as Esau's Favourite. It is a very old dish mentioned by medieval writers. Serve with a bowl of yogurt and a green salad.

4 oz whole lentils
4 tablespoons olive or cooking oil
2 large onions, chopped
salt and freshly ground black pepper
4 oz long grain rice
chicken stock or water

Soak the lentils in hot water for two hours. Drain and place in a saucepan. Just cover with more water and bring to the boil. Simmer for 35–40 minutes. Drain off any liquid into a measuring jug.

Heat the oil in another saucepan and fry the onions until they are very well browned. Add three-quarters of the onion to the lentils with the seasoning and the rice. Make the lentil liquid up to 1 pint with water or chicken stock and pour into the pan.

Bring the mixture to the boil, cover and simmer for 15–20 minutes until the rice is tender and all the liquid has been taken up. Serve topped with the remaining fried onions.

Serves 4

CHICKEN PILAF

This is a Middle-Eastern style dish and the spicing is fairly mild. Try it with lamb as a change.

1 oz butter
2 tablespoons vegetable oil
1 chicken or 4 chicken joints, cut into 8–12 pieces
salt and black pepper
1 large onion, sliced
1 clove garlic, chopped
$\frac{1}{4}$ teaspoon each ground cumin and cinnamon
pinch nutmeg
4 cardamons, crushed
1 teaspoon turmeric
8 oz long grain rice
1 pint chicken stock
2 tablespoons each raisins and flaked almonds

Heat the butter and oil in a large frying pan with a lid and brown the chicken pieces. Remove from the pan, season and keep on one side. Fry the onion, garlic and spices in the remaining fat until the onion begins to soften. Return the chicken to the pan, stir and cover. Cook slowly for 15 minutes.

Next, add the rice, stock, raisins and almonds. Bring to the boil, stir and cover the pan again. Cook for 20–30 minutes until the chicken is cooked through and the rice is tender. Add a little more stock if the dish shows signs of drying up too much.

Serves 4

ARABIAN BAKED RICE WITH VERMICELLI

This is a popular Muslim dish and may be found throughout the Middle East, and is traditionally eaten on the second night of the Muslim New Year. Serve with diced cucumber in yogurt and kebabs.

2 oz chick peas, soaked overnight
1 oz butter
1 tablespoon cooking oil
1 onion, chopped
4 oz vermicelli
6 oz long grain rice
1 pint chicken stock
2–3 cloves
salt and black pepper

Drain the chick peas, place in a pan and cover with water. Bring to the boil and cook for 40 minutes. Heat the butter and oil in a pan and fry the onion until it begins to soften. Add the vermicelli and rice and stir. Drain the chick peas and mix in with the vermicelli and rice. Transfer the mixture to a casserole. Heat the chicken stock with the cloves and seasoning and bring to the boil. Pour over the rice, stir once and bake for 40 minutes at 180C/350F/Gas 4 until all the liquid has been absorbed.

Serves 4

WESTERN RICE DISHES

VENETIAN RICE AND PEA SOUP

This dish used to be served at the banquet of the Doge of Venice on St Mark's feast day. This festival falls on 25th April when the fresh young peas from the vegetable gardens of the lagoon are just coming into season. It is a cross between a thick soup and a thin risotto.

1 oz butter
1 very small onion, finely chopped
2 oz unsmoked streaky bacon, diced
1 lb frozen petit pois
3 tablespoons freshly chopped parsley
½ teaspoon sugar
10 oz Arborio or risotto rice
2½ pints chicken stock
1 oz Parmesan cheese, grated

Heat the butter in a large saucepan and fry the onion and bacon until lightly browned. Add the peas, parsley and sugar and cook for a further 2–3 minutes. Next add the rice and stock and bring to the boil. Cover and simmer for 20 minutes. Serve sprinkled with Parmesan.

Serves 6

CHICKEN LIVER RISOTTO

This dish is fairly substantial and makes a good lunch or supper dish served with a tossed green salad.

3 oz butter
2 tablespoons cooking oil
8 oz chicken livers
1 small onion, finely chopped
8 oz Italian Arborio or risotto rice
1 small glass (5 fl oz) white wine
1 pint boiling chicken stock
salt and black pepper
3 oz Parmesan, grated

Heat 1 oz butter and 1 tablespoon oil in a frying pan and fry the chicken livers for 2–3 minutes. Drain and chop. Heat a further 1 oz butter and the rest of the oil in a saucepan and fry the onion until it turns transparent. Stir in the rice, the chicken livers and the wine. Bring to the boil and cook until all the liquid has disappeared. Add half the stock and return to the boil. Cook over a medium heat, stirring from time to time. Continue adding stock and stirring, never letting the rice dry out. Check when the rice is cooked by trying it between the teeth. The finished risotto should be creamy not runny. When the rice is cooked stir in the rest of the butter, season with salt and pepper and add a little of the cheese. Serve the rest of the cheese on the side.

Serves 4

PAELLA

Paella takes its name from the flat round frying pan with two handles which is used to cook this popular Spanish dish.

12 mussels in their shells, cleaned
4 fl oz dry white wine
1 small onion, finely chopped
2 tablespoons freshly chopped parsley
3 chicken joints, each cut into 2 or 3 pieces
4 oz chorizo or smoked sausage, sliced
4 tablespoons olive oil
1 large Spanish onion, sliced
2 cloves garlic, chopped
1 red pepper, seeded and sliced
4 large tomatoes, peeled and chopped
½ teaspoon powdered saffron
pinch cayenne pepper
12 oz risotto rice
1 pint boiling chicken stock
8 oz prawns in their shells
salt and black pepper

Cook the mussels in white wine with the chopped onion and parsley until the shells open. Keep on one side. Fry the chicken and sausage slices in half the olive oil until well browned. Remove from the pan and keep on one side.

Add the remaining oil to the pan and fry the Spanish onion, garlic and red pepper until they begin to soften. Next add the tomatoes, saffron and cayenne pepper and return the meats to the pan. Stir and add the rice and stock. Bring to the boil and cook uncovered for 15 minutes. Add the prawns and seasoning and continue cooking, covered with a lid for a further 15 minutes or until the rice is tender. Add more stock if the rice shows signs of drying up before it is cooked. Place the cooked mussels in their shells on top of the finished dish and serve.

Serves 4

HOPPING JOHN

This is a typical recipe from South Carolina.

8 oz salt pork, diced
6 oz black-eye beans, soaked overnight in cold water
1 onion, sliced
1 bayleaf
pinch of cayenne pepper
3 oz long grain rice
salt

Cook the salt pork in 1 pint of water for 30 minutes. Add the drained beans, onion, bayleaf and cayenne. Cook for 1 hour. Add the rice and simmer very gently for 20 minutes, until the rice and beans are soft and all the liquid has been absorbed. Season to taste.

Serves 4

ARROZ BRANCO

This Portuguese dish is known as nourishing rice and it certainly is a good filling dish with plenty of meat. Serve for lunch or dinner.

1 tablespoon cooking oil
6 oz lean pork, diced
6 oz lean beef, diced
4 oz gammon or lean bacon, diced
1 large onion, chopped
8 oz long grain rice
16 fl oz beef stock
2 tablespoons lemon juice
1 red pepper, seeded and cut into strips
salt and black pepper
¼ teaspoon dried thyme

Heat the cooking oil in a large saucepan and fry the diced meats until they are well sealed. Add the onion and continue frying for a further 2–3 minutes. Stir in the rice and then add the stock and the lemon juice. Bring to the boil. Stir once and then lay the pepper strips over the top. Sprinkle with seasoning and herbs. Cover with a lid and cook for 40–45 minutes until all the liquid has been absorbed.

Serves 4–6

JAMBALAYA

This recipe originates in Mississippi, and is a popular and traditional dish in the Southern States.

2 oz butter
1 tablespoon cooking oil
1 large onion, finely chopped
1 clove garlic, finely chopped
1 small green pepper, finely chopped
2 sticks celery, finely chopped
4 oz cooked ham, diced
1 x 14 oz can tomatoes
½ pint chicken stock
4 tablespoons freshly chopped parsley
pinch nutmeg
few drops Tabasco
1 teaspoon Worcestershire Sauce
8 oz long grain rice
8 oz peeled prawns
8 oz cooked chicken meat

Heat the butter and oil in a very large pan and fry the onion, garlic, green pepper, celery and ham for 2–3 minutes. Add the tomatoes and chicken stock and bring to the boil. Add all the remaining ingredients. Stir and return to the boil. Cover and cook over a very low heat for about 30 minutes until all the liquid has been absorbed and the rice is tender.

Serves 4

SPANISH RICE

This recipe actually comes from Texas but it is typical of the way in which rice is cooked throughout Mexico and South America.

4 tablespoons cooking oil
3 large onions, sliced into rings
8 oz long grain rice
salt and pepper
1/4 teaspoon mixed herbs
1/2-1 teaspoon chilli powder to taste
1 large can (1 3/4 lb) tomatoes
2 small green peppers, seeded and cut into rings
1 red pepper, seeded and cut into rings

Heat the cooking oil in a frying pan and fry the onions for 4–5 minutes. Add the rice and continue frying, stirring all the time until the rice starts to brown. Stir in the seasoning and herbs and chilli. Add all the remaining ingredients and bring to the boil. Cover with a lid and simmer for 30 minutes.

Serves 4

'They had best not stir the rice, though it sticks to the pot.'

Miguel de Cevantes 1547–1616

KEDGEREE

1 lb smoked haddock
bayleaf
2 lemons
6 peppercorns
2 oz butter
1 small onion, chopped
8 oz long grain rice
4 hard-boiled eggs, chopped
1-2 teaspoons curry powder to taste
pinch nutmeg
2 tablespoons double cream (optional)
freshly chopped parsley to garnish

Place the haddock in a saucepan with the bayleaf, 1 sliced lemon and the peppercorns. Cover with water and bring to the boil. Simmer for 5–8 minutes until the fish is tender. Drain the liquid into a measuring jug. Skin and bone the fish and keep on one side.

Heat the butter in a pan and fry the onion for 2–3 minutes. Add the rice and stir. Make the fish stock up to 16 fl oz and pour over the rice. Bring to boil. Stir and cover. Simmer for 15 minutes until the rice is cooked and all the liquid has been absorbed.

Add the flaked fish, three hard-boiled eggs, curry powder and nutmeg. Stir in the juice from the remaining lemon and cream if used. Serve garnished with the remaining chopped egg and some freshly chopped parsley.

Serves 4

RICE PUDDINGS
AND CAKES

Until recently in the West rice was probably more popular in its sweet version than as a savoury dish. But the East too has its sweet dishes made from rice.

RICE FLAKE PUDDING

1½ oz flaked rice
1 oz sugar
1½ oz dried apricots, chopped
1 pint milk

Place all the ingredients in the top of a double saucepan. Cover with a lid. Fill the base with about 2 inches of water and bring to the boil. Place the top pan into position and cook over a medium to low heat for about an hour or until the rice is cooked to your liking.

If you like the pudding fairly thick, the creamy sauce may start to separate but this does not impair the flavour. Serve hot or cold with double cream.

Serves 4

INDIAN CARDAMON PUDDING

This recipe uses long grain rice but it could be made with pudding rice for a stickier effect.

4 cardamons
½ oz butter
4 oz long grain rice
2 tablespoons flaked almonds
1 pint milk
2 oz soft brown sugar
4 tablespoons whipped cream (optional)

Remove the cardamon seeds from their pods and crush. Melt the butter and add the crushed cardamons and rice. Stir gently, and do not brown the rice. Add the flaked almonds and milk and carefully bring to the boil. Cover and simmer over a very low heat for about three-quarters of an hour until all the liquid has been absorbed. Stir in the sugar and heat through if serving hot. Otherwise leave to cool and beat in the whipped cream.

Variations include the addition of a few raisins, chopped glacé cherries or candied peel.

Serves 4

OLD-FASHIONED BAKED RICE PUDDING

1½ oz pudding rice
1½ oz sugar
1–1½ oz raisins
knob of butter
1 pint milk
½ teaspoon nutmeg

Grease an ovenproof dish and put in the dry ingredients. Add the knob of butter and pour on the milk. Sprinkle with nutmeg. Bake at 180C/350F/Gas 4 for 1 hour or until the pudding is thick enough for your taste.

Serves 4

RICE SQUARES

Proceed as for Old-Fashioned Baked Rice Pudding, but continue to cook the pudding until it is quite solid and has a cake-like consistency. Leave to cool and cut into squares. Fry the squares in very hot butter and serve sprinkled with caster sugar.

RICE SHORTCAKE

This makes a very short and crunchy biscuit which needs to be handled with care. It is delicious to eat with strong coffee and cream.

5 oz butter
4 oz self-raising flour
4 oz ground rice
2 oz soft brown sugar
pinch salt

Cream the butter with a wooden spoon until it is fairly soft. Add all the other ingredients and gradually knead together. Divide the mixture into two balls and press each one out into a small circle on a baking tray covered with greased greaseproof paper or baking parchment. The circles should be about $\frac{1}{4}$-in thick. Notch the edges with a knife handle and prick all over the centre with a fork. Bake at 180C/350F/Gas 4 for 25–30 minutes. Cut into pieces on removing from the oven and leave to cool. After 10 minutes carefully transfer to a wire rack. When completely cold store in an airtight tin.

Makes 12–16 pieces

RICE AND RAISIN BUNS

There is no wheat flour in this recipe, so the buns are suitable for anyone with an allergy to wheat. They are also very good in their own right.

3 oz butter
3 oz sugar
2 eggs, beaten
6 oz rice flour
3/4 teaspoon baking powder
1/2 teaspoon ground cinnamon
1 1/2 oz raisins

Cream the butter and sugar until it is light and fluffy. Gradually beat in the eggs, adding a little rice flour if the mixture shows signs of separating. Sift the remaining rice flour together with the baking powder and cinnamon and fold into the mixture. Then fold in the raisins. Spoon into a greased bun tray. Bake at 200C/400F/Gas 6 for 18–20 minutes until the buns are golden in colour and firm in the centre. Remove from the bun tray and leave to cool on a wire rack.

Makes 15

'Sorrow is like rice in the store: a basketful removed every day, it comes to an end at last.' Malagasy Proverb